Your parents are cool

For Alexa, the coolest thing I've ever done.

This book is for you,
dear child,
A glimpse of our life
when we were wild.

Before routines, diapers,
bottles, and drool,
Before kids came along,
your parents were cool.

We loved to party
before you were born,
Nightclubs, dance floors,
home at dawn.

Dancing to the beat,
we were young and free,
How life got serious
when two became three.

We would hit the bars for
cocktails and beers,
Laugh hysterically until
there were tears.

These days it's your formula being
shaken, not stirred,
While our days are long,
and our nights are blurred.

Dining at the hippest
restaurants in the city,
Our reservation at nine,
it was loud and busy.

Food is now served at six,
the menus mundane,
What happened to lobster,
carpaccio, and champagne?

Conversations so deep,
we lost track of time,
Nights around a table with
food, friends, and wine.

Now all we speak about is
the mess on the floor,
The attention on Dora and
all she'll explore.

The world was our oyster,
spontaneity - our friend,
Never having to worry when
the adventure would end.

We drank buckets in Thailand,
ate churros in Spain,
Will there ever be a holiday
without a kids' club again?

We would get on a plane
and leave stress behind,
Sit back, relax, exhale,
and unwind.

Baby, the plane ride is now a
pain in the rear,
As you constantly cry and
whine in our ear.

Saturdays spent shopping
for the sublime,
Marc Jacobs, Armani, and
Calvin Klein.

Indulgent purchases on
Prada and Jimmy Choo,
Now our hottest accessory is
definitely you.

I know it's hard for
you to believe,
Your parents had a life before
you were conceived.

Trust me kid,
we weren't always delirious,
We were calm and cool,
when life was less serious.

Darling, you arrived and
are as cute as they come,
With you, we enjoy a
different kind of fun.

you're invited to
Giulia & Daryls

Cocktail
Party

saturday may 8th
drinks, dinner & dancing

Moments as a family is now
what we treasure,
Our partying days,
a rare and wonderful pleasure.

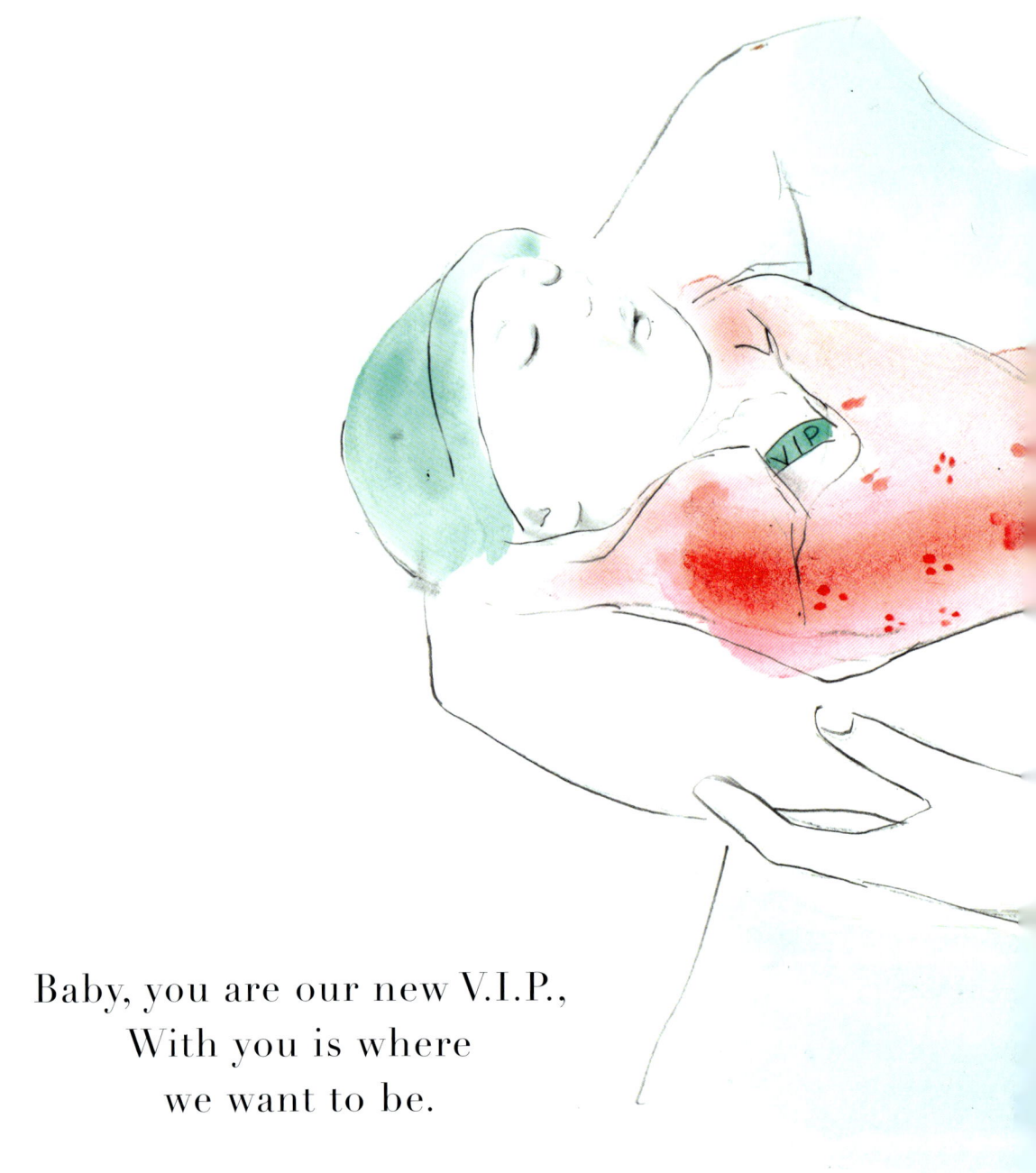

Baby, you are our new V.I.P.,
With you is where
we want to be.

The coolness over? How untrue!
We didn't know what cool was
until we had you.

About Giulia...

Giulia Ferrari is a Melbourne based writer and teacher, ex party girl, avid traveller, wife, and now a MOTHER!

After her daughter Alexa arrived, Ferrari would find herself on the phone laughing (sometimes crying) to her friends about how life had changed.

Giulia quickly learned that the fun was definitely not over... in fact, it had only just begun.

Connect with Giulia:
ig | fb @yourparentsarecool
www.yourparentsarecool.com

About Sarah...

Sarah Hankinson captures the pulse of modern style with her classic illustrations, which pair soft splashes of colours and meticulous line work to portray control and impulse, form and silhouette. Her work balances light and dark to create elegant illustrations drawn with a harmonious combination of traditional and mixed media techniques.

Some of Sarah's clients include *Harper's Bazaar Magazine*, Maybelline New York-Austraila, and US Target.

Connect with Sarah:
ig | fb @sarahhankinsonillustration
www.sarahhankinsonillustration.com

Locking arms and helping each other down their Golden Brick Road

At Golden Brick Road Publishing House, we lock arms with ambitious people and create success through a collaborative, supportive, and accountable environment. We are a boutique shop that caters to all stages of business around a book. We encourage women empowerment, and gender and cultural equality by publishing single author works from around the world, and creating in-house collaborative author projects for emerging and seasoned authors to join.

Our authors have a safe space to grow and diversify themselves within the genres of poetry, health, sociology, women's studies, business, and personal development. We help those who are natural born leaders, step out and shine! Even if they do not yet fully see it for themselves. We believe in empowering each individual who will then go and inspire an entire community. Our Director, Ky-Lee Hanson, calls this The Inspiration Trickle Effect. If you want to be a public figure that is focused on helping people and providing value, but you do not want to embark on the journey alone, then we are the community for you.

To inquire about our collaborative writing opportunities or to bring your own idea into vision, reach out to us at www.goldenbrickroad.pub

 Society

Goals, Brilliance and Reinvention

Join us at the social

www.gbrsociety.com

GBR Society is a safe space to bring everyone together (authors, future authors, readers, and supporters) in an academy-like setting; making social media a productive tool focused on practical learning, growth, and friendships. Think of it like a super positive and intellectual online sorority house. Join us and create positive friendships as you flex your skills and learn new ones.

We take part in many charitable events, host retreats, and focus on making reading and self-development cool and fun.

See you at the social!